MW00776358

REFLECTIONS OF AN EDITOR

INSIGHTS & OBSERVATIONS OF A SMALL-TOWN NEWSMAN

ART HADDAWAY

REFLECTIONS OF AN EDITOR:
INSIGHTS & OBSERVATIONS OF A SMALL-TOWN NEWSMAN

First Edition: February, 2022
ISBN: 978-1-7351818-1-3 (Paperback)
ISBN: 978-1-7351818-2-0 (Hardback)

Contains previously published works by Art Haddaway in the Owasso Reporter between Oct. 2016 and Jan. 2022 with permission from Lee Enterprises.

Title page photo by Dillon Watkins of *Captures by Dillon Lee.*

Design Vault Press, LLC
www.designvaultpress.com

To my parents, who raised me right; my church family, who embraced me; my close friends, who stuck with me; and the residents of Owasso, who made this book possible.

TABLE OF CONTENTS

INTRODUCTION

When I wrote my first editorial column upon starting at Owasso Reporter over six years ago, I couldn't have imagined that it would eventually lead to a book deal.

A short piece introducing myself to residents of a town I knew little about turned into dozens of heartfelt letters to those same residents who have become close friends and colleagues of a town I now call home.

This book is a collection of many of these columns.

The idea to compile these personal narratives into a published collection has always been a longtime goal, but it wasn't until the COVID-19 pandemic that I knew I needed to pursue this passion project sooner than later.

A historic time of civil unrest and political divisiveness served as a grim reminder of the need for a clear, calming voice amid the chaos.

Enter "Reflections of an Editor."

This four-part anthology features different insights and observations from my time as editor of the Owasso Reporter, each entry carrying the same positive undertone as its first appearance in the newspaper's editorial pages.

Formatted as a devotional of sorts, this handbook is meant

to inform, inspire, educate and entertain. It's meant to uplift and to enrich. It's meant to exhort and to challenge.

Part 1, "A Little Heart, A Little Humor" gives readers a light-hearted skim through various topics before steering them into the realm of the media in Part 2, "Pieces of the Press." They can then turn their attention toward spirituality and community in Part 3, "Faith, Fellowship & Fortitude," and then round the final corner into Part 4, "An Ode to Owasso" spotlighting Tulsa's northernmost neighboring suburb.

Those not inclined to flip through a chronological read can also randomly peruse the book at their leisure.

Regardless of how local bookworms browse these pages, they'll be met with a unique telling of a small-town editor's experiences — and the life lessons he's learned — during his time at the keyboard, behind the camera lens and around others in the community that he loves the most.

May these intimate chronicles — devoutly written in times of both happiness and heartbreak — bring joy, hope, revelation and renewal, along with important values to carry into the days, weeks, months and years ahead.

Art Haddaway

1

A LITTLE HEART, A LITTLE HUMOR

1:1

RESCUER OF REPAIRS,
COWBOY OF CONSTRUCTION

(OR NOT)

Be content in who you are, confident in what you do and contagious in the passion you possess.

I'm not your average "hands-on" guy. In fact, I'm far from it.

Walk into my storage closet and you'll find a scarce tool collection consisting of a hammer, some nails and screws, a pair of pliers, a wrench for God knows what and a tape measure — a sad sight indeed.

But I try to make up for it in other ways.

I've always had a knack for the written word. It started early on when I accepted a position as a copy editor for my high school newspaper. It wasn't Pulitzer-winning material, but I took pride in what I put to print.

I then set my sights on college, where I grabbed a journalism degree, freelanced for any publication that would accept my desperate pleas, and eventually landed a full-time job in my chosen field, which set me on the path I am today.

It's been 20 years of putting pen to paper, so to speak. Oh the hours and hours spent in front of a screen pouring heart and soul into story after story. All that time behind a desk has led to a perfected craft, but not one to impress Chip Gaines or Bob Vila.

When your home is in disrepair, when you're in need of that heroic handy man, I'm not your guy. No, my contribution to society comes by telling you where to place a comma or when to use a hyphen — cue the earth-shattering excitement.

I, of course, find that enthralling, but at the end of the day, it's not going to help fix your sink or rewire your thermostat (is that even a thing?). Adding that comma or hyphen won't make that much of a difference in the grand scheme of things.

Does the world need more journalists, or are plumbers and electricians in higher demand? Perhaps it's in need of journalists who write about plumbers and electricians. Who's to say? All I know is I have the thing I'm good at and they have theirs, and the world continues to revolve.

Sometimes I wish I held a different title, one that painted me as the rescuer of repairs or the cowboy of construction, but I always come back to what the good Lord has bestowed upon me, and that's the ability to tell their stories, not mirror them.

I've learned that comparing myself to others, especially those who are more adept at handling those "hands-on" projects, could lead to discontentment, jealousy or resentment.

Be content in who you are, confident in what you do and contagious in the passion you possess. Whether you're a plumber or an electrician, or a writer who can't tell the difference between a wrench and a pair of pliers, you should don your title proudly for all to see.

REFLECTION

How are you focusing on the talents you do have, rather than those you don't? Accept what you're good at and work toward improving yourself in those areas.

1:2
COFFEE: A TRUE ALLY IN TIMES OF TROUBLE

It (coffee) reassures, rejuvenates,
becalms and beautifies.

In the newspaper business, there are three things every reporter can't go without when writing a successful story: facts, coffee and more coffee.

Call it what you will — the "writer's brew," the "journalist's java" the "columnist's cappuccino" — but coffee holds a special place in the hearts of many people in the press.

A recent study by UK-based media distribution firm Pressat shows that out of 10,000 professionals surveyed, those in the news industry were found to drink the most coffee at more than four cups per day.

This is a sizable statistic, but one that doesn't surprise me. There are few media folk I've met in my career who don't share the same sentiment toward the drink, and I'm proud to be a part of those who do.

For those of us plugging away behind the screen under deadline and full of drive, coffee takes the edge off and gets those creative juices flowing. Simply put, it reassures, rejuvenates, becalms and beautifies.

There's never an article I write, never a paragraph I revise, never a page I layout without a hot cup of dark roast by my side. In fact, much of what you read in these pages is complemented by the caffeinated beverage.

To quote the wise words of French novelist and playwright Honoré de Balzac, "As soon as coffee is in your stomach, there is a general commotion. Ideas begin to move ... similes arise, the paper is covered. Coffee is your ally, and writing ceases to be a struggle."

REFLECTION

*W*hat's your "coffee"? What helps you overcome challenges? Find something (anything from a rhyme or song to a
book or keepsake) that helps you get through the day.*

1:3

WE'RE SMALL
BUT NOT INSIGNIFICANT

You're you, and that's all that matters.

recently discovered a new app that I can't put down.
  It's called Flightradar24, and it allows you to track every active flight in the world in real-time on a detailed map. Yes, you heard me right: every flight.

It shows everything from flight numbers to trip origins and destinations to aircraft altitudes, headings and speeds. You can even zoom in and watch each plane as it flies through the air.

How cool is that?

Sometimes I'll just scan the sky and look for a plane overhead so I can grab my phone and track what kind of aircraft it is and where it's going. It's quite a distraction, really.

Call me a nerd, but I find it fascinating that we now have

the technology to, at the flick of a finger, pull up and view what I assume air traffic controllers see on a daily basis. It's literally a radar screen on the go.

For those who know me well, I've always been obsessed with airplanes and aerodynamics. There's just something about a 600-ton tube filled with dozens of people flying through the air at a high rate of speed that never stops intriguing me.

In fact, my dream job (aside from being a New York Times bestselling author, of course) is to be a commercial pilot. Oh to sit in that cockpit, press all those shiny buttons and see the world through the eyes of "the captain."

But I digress.

I guess the reason why an app like Flightradar24 often steals my attention — aside from it being such a satisfying time-waster — is because it reminds me just how big the world is and how small and seemingly insignificant we really are.

The latter, however, couldn't be farther from the truth.

With thousands of us passing each other on the highways in the sky each day going every which way across the globe, it's easy to blend in as another face in the crowd, another passenger in a window seat, another sprinter to a connecting flight.

But you're more than just a hurried traveler. You're a mom, a dad, a son, a daughter; a school teacher, a business owner, a city official, a construction worker. You're someone of importance, regardless of your title or profession.

You're you, and that's all that matters.

Watching all those tiny, yellow plane icons span the map on Flightracker24 inspires me to write something reminding my readers that, while small, they're not in the least insignificant.

So the next time you see a plane overhead, grab your phone, pull up the app and be mindful of all those onboard.

There's a good chance someone in a window seat is looking down on you thinking the same thing.

REFLECTION

*W*hy do you sometimes feel insignificant? In what ways can you combat those thoughts? Remind yourself that you are, in fact, significant.

1:4
A MUG WORTH KEEPING AROUND THE DESK

*I should have acknowledged a long time ago
(that) I need to give myself more grace.*

Back in Oct. 2016, my amazing staff (when I had a full team) bought me a new mug with the words "World's Best Boss" stamped on the side. It was quite a pleasant surprise, as I thoroughly enjoy collecting mugs (half my desk is donned with them).

However, I didn't — and still don't — consider myself the "World's Best Boss"; I feel a more accurate representation would be the "World's Best Stickler" or the "World's Best Workaholic." While I'm not proud of these phrases, I can better identify with them.

I truly appreciate my team's inscribed perception of me, especially now that I'm reminded of it on a daily basis during my regular coffee runs to and from the kitchen. What's more, their kind gesture has taught me something I should have acknowledged a long time ago: I need to give myself more grace.

I often find myself focusing more on the negative and what I don't do right, rather than on the positive and what I do right. They say old habits die hard, and this is one pattern of thinking that has remained unbroken for quite some time.

This mentality comes from the shame of living imperfectly — whether it's misspeaking during a meeting, overlooking a typo after a story prints or not knowing the right answer to an important question — and I'm realizing how this can hinder my pursuit of a healthy lifestyle.

Despite these pretenses, I'm learning how to put my best foot forward and finish each day on a strong note with a good attitude, regardless of how flawless I perform. This means I need to allow myself to loosen up, laugh more and, of course, enjoy more coffee.

The phrase "World's Best Boss" doesn't necessarily reflect the characteristics of one who always has it all together. It simply serves as a humble reminder that I have remarkable colleagues — and friends — who still support me despite my imperfections.

REFLECTION

In what areas do you struggle with perfectionism? How are you breaking down the walls of perfectionism in your own life?

1:5
TAKE TIME TO GET LOST
IN A GOOD SHOW

Get cozy ... kick off a good TV series and immerse yourself in another world.

Everyone has "their show."

At one time or another, we've all laid claim to that binge-worthy program we can't stop watching — and talking about — with friends, family or co-workers.

We grow attached to the environments, the characters and their personalities, the storylines, the narratives, the conflicts, the art and visuals and more.

There's something about getting caught up in a world where others' tragedies and triumphs overshadow our own, making us laugh and cry, gasp in shock, seethe with anger, gripe with disappointment or cheer for joy.

But why is this realm of entertainment so captivating to

us? What is the draw? How does a particular TV series get so popular? And why does it affect our lives in such profound ways?

With a seemingly endless range of streaming services nowadays, it's easier than ever to tune into any show at any time from the comfort of our own couch. Whatever your genre of choice, it's all there at the press of button.

Skeptics may claim that instant accessibility to an unlimited number of titles has negative consequences, with excessive viewing inducing laziness or leading to a "dumbing down" of society. For the most part, however, I disagree.

I've always been drawn to TV shows. Becoming part of someone else's story, tapping into their emotions, experiencing the world from their point of view, has kept me coming back to the big screen time after time — and it's not a bad thing.

A good screenplay inspires and encourages, breaks down cultural and societal barriers, helps heal old wounds, awakens desires, releases stress and anxiety, arouses delight, the list goes on and on. What's more, a well-written script does what it's intended to do: entertain.

Despite what some may say, I believe entertainment — particularly television — is essential to our well-being. Sure, left unchecked, consuming an overabundance of content could have harmful effects, but overall it's a necessary escape from some of life's inevitable stresses.

Some of my personal favorites include: "24," "Breaking Bad," "The Walking Dead," "Lost," "House" and "Prison Break."

As for some comedies, I suggest: "The Office," "Parks and Recreation," "New Girl," "Friends" and "Arrested Development."

I also thoroughly enjoy a good docuseries or survival show like "Making a Murderer" and "The Staircase," as well as "Survivorman" and "I Shouldn't Be Alive."

Get cozy on the couch, kick off a good TV series and immerse yourself in another world where the realities of this one fade away.

REFLECTION

*D*o you prioritize relaxation in front of a screen? Do you allow yourself to get lost in a TV show? If not, perhaps it's time to meander off course just a bit.

1:6
THE RUSTIC, RUGGED FEEL OF A FIRE

My eyes gazed on the glory of a new wood-burning basin.

My now ex-wife and I moved into a new house back in Oct. 2017. It was a rental, mind you, but we took it over our previous quarters: a cramped, two-bedroom apartment.

Our new abode was spacious, homey and full of life, and it fit us just right. It was everything we could have wanted in a house, and more, meaning there was a small fire pit left in the backyard with my name written all over it.

Now remember, we just came from a tiny apartment with a strict "no burn" policy, so when my eyes gazed on the glory of a new wood-burning basin, I was ecstatic to say the least.

I'd be lying if I said I was an avid outdoorsman, but I at least aspire to make something of my surroundings when I can, and apartment life certainly didn't cater to this endeavor. With a new home, however, that was a different story.

Cutting the grass, trimming the bushes and even sweeping the garage — all somewhat foreign concepts to me in an apartment — were now helping to beef up my machismo. And creating fire, well that was an added bonus.

A fire pit provided an opportunity for me to step up my game on the nature scene and learn new tricks of the trade when it came to, you guessed it, making a fire.

I was eager to get my hands dirty — literally — learning about everything from the basics of wood gathering to the usage of tinder and kindling to the different techniques of fire building.

We were in the new house for only a month, and I had already used the fire pit more times than I could count. As a beginner, I felt I was off to a good start.

There's just something about hunkering down by the rustic, rugged feel of a fire and soaking up that thick, smoky scent that brings you back to a sense of the wild, even if it's in your backyard.

And while I may never be considered a true outdoorsman by society's standards, I like to think I donned somewhat of a new identity through the brief time at that home: wood-gatherer, ax-wielder and fire-maker.

REFLECTION

What new skill have you picked up that has contributed to a new or renewed identity for you? How have you continued to improve on that skill?

1:7
DRESSING THE PART
FOR ANY EVENT

*It's advantageous to don an outfit that reflects
success from time to time.*

Growing up, I was taught to dress for the job you want, not the job you have — sage advice for a young lad looking to get ahead in the world.

These priceless words of wisdom have continued to stick with me in donning different apparel throughout my working years.

Whether it's an interview, networking event or speaking engagement, I always strive to dress with excellence for every occasion. Of course, in the latter years of my profession, I've grown comfortable sporting a casual ensemble of jeans and an untucked, button-down shirt.

Now, I don't mean to come across haughty; I simply want

to share how much I enjoy putting on a suit and tie (which nowadays isn't often).

Graduating college in 2008 — and before settling into my journalism career — I was fortunate enough to land a job at Men's Wearhouse as a customer service associate. Over the next four years, I worked my way up to a wardrobe consultant and eventually the operations manager for a store in Arkansas.

I learned everything I needed to know about men's fashion and the importance of modeling the best attire where appropriate. Blues versus greys, stripes against solids, peaks over shawls: These were the day-to-day quandaries I faced — and still do — but with ease thanks to what I learned in retail.

Are there times I'm overdressed? I'm sure. Do I dress down on occasion for the heck of it? Absolutely. Am I the poster boy for GQ? Definitely not. My point is I've found that it's advantageous to don an outfit that reflects success from time to time.

While there are worse issues to be concerned with, I'm thankful I was raised in a household that taught me the value of dressing well and embracing the opportunities it brings.

REFLECTION

Go through your closet and find something a little more up-scale today. You never know what heads you'll turn.

2
PIECES OF THE PRESS

2:1
THE IMPORTANCE
OF US MEDIA FOLK

'Journalism is storytelling with a purpose.'

attended a dinner party a few years back with some close friends, where we engaged in a conversation about everything from the global financial crisis to religious practices to the inauguration of Donald Trump.

One friend asked me several questions about my role in covering these different subjects — how the media operates, its role in society today, where it's going and more.

This ultimately led him to pose a rather thought-provoking question: "Why, when it comes down to it, does news matter? Why is it important?"

I wish I could say I responded with a profound, philosophical answer full of colorful words to describe its obvious relevance, but I kept it simple: "We're here to give people the content that's important to them."

Of course, I added a few more remarks to my retort, but I emphasized that much of the public yearns to be engaged, informed and entertained, and the media can play a large part in fulfilling that.

In the book, "The Elements of Journalism," authors Bill Kovach and Tom Rosenstiel reference what's called the "Awareness Instinct." This suggests that people desire to be aware of what's happening outside their own lives for the sake of satisfying their curiosities.

The book states, "… News satisfies a basic human impulse. People have an intrinsic need — and instinct — to know what is occurring beyond their direct experience. Being aware of events we cannot see for ourselves engenders a sense of security, control and confidence."

Beyond awareness, the public longs to feel valued, grasp onto inspiration and connect to others on a deeper emotional and spiritual level. The media can offer up stories to strike a chord with readers or viewers looking for these very attributes.

As Kovach and Rosenstiel say, "Journalism is storytelling with a purpose … to provide people with information they need to understand the world. The first challenge is finding the information that people need to live their lives. The second is to make it meaningful, relevant and engaging."

However, the public's ongoing need to receive coverage

that matters to them should also be met with honest, accurate reporting from the very outlets that provide that coverage.

People should settle for nothing less than fair, factual, non-fabricated content; otherwise, it defeats the purpose of why the media exists in the first place: to publish the cold, hard truth regardless of the topic at hand (with the exception of editorials, of course).

At the end of the day, news creates itself; we're just here to fill the public in on what happened and what's to come. Simply put, the purpose of the media is to ensure that those who seek — and expect — relevant, relatable and responsible stories continue to receive them.

REFLECTION

*W*hy is it important for you to be informed and engaged? Develop a desire to grow more knowledgeable about local happenings and national/worldwide events.

2:2
TAKING THE TIME TO TALK 'OFF THE RECORD'

The art of small talk is an overlooked practice
that could always be perfected.

U s media folk are a persistent bunch.
Whether we're listening in at a city meeting, talking with students at a local school or recording details at the scene of a crime, newsgathering is priority No. 1.

We're commonly seen across the community — a recorder and camera in hand — navigating through crowds and asking pressing questions to get the inside scoop on the most important stories of the day.

Words like "eager," "hurried," "restless" or "deadline-driven" are often used to paint our personalities, and there's no doubt I live up to those stereotypes, sometimes more than I care to admit.

In fact, I joke that journalists would make the best and worst superheroes: We'd be the first ones on scene, but we'd stop to ask what happened rather than jump to rescue those in need.

I can't help but wonder of the dozens of people I "interrogate" on a weekly basis — city officials, business owners, school staff, public safety officials or just the average Joe — how many actually look forward to the conversation or run to the hills in an attempt to escape.

Most of my beloved sources know my routine by now: Snap a few pictures, hit record, ask a question or two and break away to publish the big story. I'm "that guy." And I hold true to that title unapologetically.

It goes without saying that as "that guy," my job — my responsibility as a journalist to report the news accurately and fairly — is to go "on the record." Heck, most of my day is spent "on the record." It's a core belief among us reporters, a foundational truth, an innate characteristic, ingrained in each of us, unceasing in our coverage.

Going "on the record" is what we as the press do, and we do it proudly.

There is, however, one important thing I'm continuing to discern: when and where to go "off the record" (insert audible gasps from my media counterparts here).

Yes, I've broached a taboo subject. The phrase "off the record" is a dirty word in the media world. Again, it goes against everything we stand for. The drive, the hunt, to capture the perfect quote, the compelling statement, the inspirational speech, is an integral part of who we are.

So what do I mean when I say go "off the record"? For me, it's removing the reporter hat, shutting off the recorder and taking a few moments to make small talk with someone with no strings attached.

Time is money in the dog-eat-dog world of journalism, and much of mine is spent typing away behind a screen against deadline — and rightfully so. But there's no doubt that devoting an extra minute or two to shoot the breeze with a source before or after an interview goes a long way.

Sure, you'll find us newsies at a number of events smiling, shaking hands and conversing with the crowd with no equipment in hand, but I still feel the art of small talk is an overlooked practice that could always be perfected.

What's more, as one who mainly identifies as an introvert, it's easy for me to hide behind a camera or a pen and paper when there's a specific timetable or agenda; there's a familiar sense of solace when donning that press pass.

Thankfully venturing into the treacherous territory of undocumented conversation has become easier for me over the years — largely in part to the affable residents of Owasso who have helped me hone those communication skills.

Going "off the record" is a foreign concept to me and many of my media brethren. It's challenging, it's uncomfortable, and most of all, it's uncertain. But I'd also be unwise not to.

REFLECTION

*D*o you have an agenda — a "record-keeping" system — when conversing with others? Take time to get to know others without an ulterior motive.

2:3
PUBLIC DISCOURSE:
THE LIFEBLOOD OF NEWSPAPERS

Constructive discourse, when facilitated by an objective medium, paves the way for a productive society.

Any journalist will tell you that the editorial pages of a newspaper serve as the lifeblood of the publication.

The section features a range of content, from personal columns to letters to the editor, that gives readers an outlet to express their viewpoints in a constructive manner. This long-standing tradition is ingrained in the foundation of community journalism.

Varying opinions and diverse thoughts about local, national and global issues are put to print for citizens to either commend or criticize.

In 2020, for example, there was certainly no shortage of material — with letters to the editor, in particular — piling up in the wake of COVID-19, covering topics like Oklahoma's social restrictions and Trump's handling of the pandemic.

These letters came in many forms, some more boisterous or opinionated than others, espousing rhetoric from both sides of the aisle, in an attempt to inform or persuade audiences alike. We always welcome any and all feedback from the public, and these opinions are as valid as the ones they're scrutinizing.

However, letters to the editor are published as opinions and do not reflect the viewpoints of the newspaper staff. Our role is to provide a forum for this dissenting commentary within the confines of the editorial pages.

Anything to the contrary would, in fact, go against our role — our fundamental responsibility — as objective journalists. We would be doing the community a disservice if we didn't give a voice to those who have one, which is, after all, the primary purpose of a newspaper.

In a 2003 article released by Poynter, John Taylor, editorial page editor of the Wilmington (Del.) News-Journal, is quoted, "'I publish (letters to the editor) because I think it deserves publication, even though it's on the edge.' The danger of offending readers, Taylor says, is 'far outweighed by the service that you do letting ... your reading public and the public at large know that this viewpoint ... is a real viewpoint and it exists in the community.'"

Jack Wilson, editorial page editor of the Eugene (Ore.) Register-Guard, is also referenced as saying, "'There's some value in providing readers with a notion of what people in their community are saying and thinking ... We do our best to maintain a kind of a coarse filter and err on the side of publishing something rather than not publishing it.'"

Some have argued that we only share or publish those letters that align with our own political agendas; I can assure you the opposite is true. Our vetting process is not based on partisanship, but impartiality.

What comes across our desks is what you see. One week, we may only receive a left-leaning letter; other weeks, it may steer toward the right. Frankly, I feel we don't receive enough correspondence on the regular — a lost art in the age of the war of words on social media.

I encourage the community to submit more of their thoughts to their local newspaper, but also their rebuttals of those ideologies. Constructive discourse, when facilitated by an objective medium, paves the way for a productive society.

REFLECTION

Is there an issue you care about and want to share with others in a constructive way? I encourage you to submit a letter to the editor to your local newspaper.

2:4
THE TRUE, CHARMING
NATURE OF PUNCTUATION

These symbols, working together, create the symphony of the paragraph.

Allow me take this time to broach a subject near and dear to my heart: punctuation. Yes, what most people regard as a nerdy nuisance, I esteem as a timeless treasure.

Many often consider punctuation boring, mechanical and lifeless, and I don't blame them. There are many rules to remember and they can be quite confusing at times. However, the opposite is true when you pull back the curtain and reveal the true, charming nature of punctuation and how it behaves on the page.

In his book, "A Dash of Style: The Art and Mastery of Punctuation," author Noah Lukeman describes punctuation as more of an art form rather than just a facilitator for sentences.

"Rarely is (punctuation) pondered as a medium for artistic expression, as a means of impacting the content … where it achieves symbiosis with narration, style, viewpoint, and even the plot itself," he says.

Lukeman gives relatable, lifelike and rather entertaining characteristics to those punctuation marks most commonly used in English writing today.

For example: The period is the stop sign of the punctuation world; the comma serves as the speed bump in the sentence; the semicolon acts as the bridge on the wordy road; the colon is the magician, revealing key information; the dash serves as the interrupter of the conversation; the parentheses act as the advisors of a thought; and quotation marks are the trumpets of the passage.

He goes on to discuss the question mark, exclamation point, italics, ellipses, the hyphen and more, each enlivening the page with their own unique personalities.

Lukeman no doubt provides a newfound and intriguing perspective on those pesky punctuation marks no one seems to pay much attention to while skimming the story.

The author goes even further to say there's an underlying rhythm to all text, and punctuation is the music of the language. These symbols, working together, create the symphony of the paragraph.

But punctuation is more than just a melody — it's a live, breathing source of creativity. These symbols exist in a realm of heightened activity "like a world of microorganisms living in a pond ... teeming with life," as Lukeman puts it.

"Ultimately, the end result of any work is only as good as the method in getting there, and there is no way there without these strange dots and lines and curves we call punctuation," he says.

REFLECTION

*P*ause and admire the ebb and flow of punctuation the next time you read a news article or pick up a book; it's quite a creative infrastructure to behold.

2:5
FAKE STORIES:
THE NEW NORM OF THE NEWS?

Fast-forward to today, and little has changed in the way of headlines and hearsay.

Former President Donald Trump said in a recent press conference that he will take up smoking to help ease stress. On a related note, Hilary Clinton said she will do the same, claiming to be inspired by Trump's decision.

The two will soon meet in the White House Rose Garden with President Joe Biden, where they will share a friendly smoke and reminisce about their experiences running against each other in 2016 presidential election.

This, of course, is a rather humorous example of "fake" news — a story contrived by Yours Truly for the sake of misleading you to believe something that simply isn't true. I wish I could say, however, this brief is just a one-time fabrication, but sadly, I stand incorrect.

In the wake of what seemed to be the most controversial election in our nation's history, the public was — and continues to be — inundated with a number of bogus articles from across the internet and social media. Many have gone viral and have even been picked up by the mainstream media.

Fast-forward to today, and little has changed in the way of headlines and hearsay. The rumored rhetoric of former candidates has been replaced with convoluted conversations about masks, vaccines, voter fraud and the like.

According to the Pew Research Center, about two-in-three U.S. adults (64% of 1,002 surveyed) said they believe fake stories like these have caused much confusion about the basic facts of current issues. It also showed that 23% of them said they have shared at least one fabricated article whether they knew it or not.

These are staggering statistics that prove these stories, in my opinion, have misled and misinformed millions around the country and across the globe. What's more, they have insulted the intelligence of readers and viewers, disgraced the ethics of true journalism and ultimately posed a danger to society as a whole.

It goes without saying that a number of media outlets today embellish the facts or fabricate their stories for the sake of ratings and readership — a popularity contest, if you will. To quote the wise words of Albert Einstein: "What is right is not always popular, and what is popular is not always right."

I'm against sensationalism and refuse to give in to this trend that seems to be the "new norm" for the news industry.

Those numbers from Pew, as detrimental as they are, serve as a valuable reminder for true journalists to continue providing the public with factual, accurate and objective content.

REFLECTION

How are you vetting your news sources? Find and stick with those reputable reporters and news outlets that don't have an agenda (there are many still out there).

2:6
A BREAK FROM THE NEWS ISN'T ALL THAT BAD

*These mental meanderings are here to offer the
newsgathering public a bit of respite.*

A cold bottle of root beer, some upbeat trance tunes and a warm, sunny day is all the inspiration I need to write yet another column.

No, I'm not lounging on a scenic beach in the Bahamas. I'm sitting at my desk, sipping my A&W and glancing out the window with my headphones in. But that's enough to spur me on to type out my innermost thoughts.

These mental meanderings are here to offer the newsgathering public a bit of respite amid the constant inundation of "who wronged who," "where this event is being held" and "what bill is being signed and when."

Contrary to my role as a journalist to seek out that infor-

mation, this commenatary simply serves as a quick breather —
a pause, a timeout, a much-needed interruption — from the
never-ending news cycle.

So here's something to chew on other than that breaking
release you've been dying to read:

A few years ago, I ventured down to Broken Bow and rent-
ed a cabin deep in the wooded terrain of Beaver's Bend State
Park. It was my first adventure down there, and it certainly
won't be my last.

My cabin was uniquely nicknamed "Unwind," and I can
see why. My retreat mainly consisted of nothing except unwind-
ing — either on the porch, by the fire pit or inside the hot tub.

Just picture yourself taking in the clean, crisp air amid the
quiet, quaint property nestled underneath a canopy of rustling
pines surrounded by the solitude of the wild. The only question
you're asking is, "When do I leave?"

See, three paragraphs later, and you already want to drop
everything and go unplug from the world.

I could go on and on about my trip and how rejuvenating
it was, but I digress.

My job is to bring you information, but it's also to take you
away from it from time to time, and instead, offer you a fresh
perspective (hence the reference to the comfy cabin). After all,
that's what the editorial pages are for, right?

There's a time and a place for everything, and I hope
the last two minutes it took you to read this column was time

well spent removed from the news to have that much-needed breather. Remember to carry that into your everyday regimen going forward.

REFLECTION

*D*o you find yourself searching and scrolling through the vast array of endless headlines? Pause, breath and enjoy venturing to a picturesque place of respite for a bit.

2:7

COW BELLS, HAND CLAPPERS AND LOUD CHEERS

These were career-high moments that will forever be etched into our memories.

Cow bells, glittered hand clappers and loud cheers. These are all the makings for an entertaining evening.

Such has been the case at Oklahoma Press Association's annual convention over the last several years.

The event, hosted every June in or near Oklahoma City, plays host to a full program of engaging workshops and sessions over a two-day period, and culminates in the most anticipated hour for local newspaper teams across the state: the venerated awards banquet.

There, dozens of journalists, editors and publishers gather in a central location to celebrate the previous year's best stories and photos and most notable accomplishments.

The contest pits 75 Oklahoma newspapers against each other in a friendly competition that leaves them eagerly awaiting the name of their publication to be announced for first, second or third place in a handful of categories, including news content, feature writing, advertising, layout & design and more.

Add to that delicious food, fun conversation among staff members and gobs of celebratory gear (like those cow bells and hand clappers) and you have an evening worth remembering.

I'm proud to say that during my time at the helm of Owasso Reporter, my former team (now me, myself and I) have brought home about 40 awards in the last six years from the prestigious event.

Donning our best suits and ties and elegant gowns, we took to the stage with big smiles and high spirits as the large crowd cheered us on. It goes without saying that these were career-high moments that will forever be etched into our memories.

A lot has happened in the Owasso community during my stint as editor that has warranted much in-depth coverage — and, apparently, that has caught the eyes of our best critics.

OPA's anticipated annual event, however, offers more than just another plaque or certificate to add to my wall (although it is getting quite cluttered). It's an opportunity to thank my dedicated readers for their continued support.

Every week, local subscribers return to the paper for another story, another picture, another column, to stay informed, up-to-date, inspired, engaged. Heck, some pick it up just for the crossword puzzle. Without them, I wouldn't have an opportunity to celebrate the paper's accomplishments.

REFLECTION

*H*ere's a simple "thank you" for being a part of a community that continues to support local news and recognizes its importance.

2:8
REFLECTING ON COVERING
THE PANDEMIC

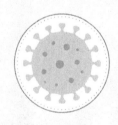

I've learned to be kinder, to count my blessings, to embrace change and to lend a listening ear to (others).

In 2020, all of our lives changed as the pandemic became a prominent front-page story across the world.

The news was unexpected and unprecedented — a historic turn of events that, unbeknownst to us at the time, would ultimately reshape how we live, interact with others and perceive the world.

I remember leading our March 18, 2020, paper with the headline, "Area schools shut down," followed by another, "City closes restaurants, bars," in the following week's edition. It was at that point I knew our coverage would never look the same going forward.

Those stories would grow from two to nearly 200 over the

next 12 months. That averages to about three to four articles per week. I've written the majority of those, covering everything from city-wide cases and hospital stats to vaccination updates and school district quarantine rates.

To say I'm familiar with the state of the coronavirus on the local front would be an understatement. That's not a pretentious assertion, just a reminder that I'm overdue for a much-needed vacation (but aren't we all).

I've been asked questions like, "How has it been covering the coronavirus?" "What's changed in the newsroom?" "Where do you find the time to jump from one story to the next?" I relish answering these because it's a pivotal time to be a journalist in today's climate. Now more than ever, people are in need of real, objective, trustworthy news.

Covering the pandemic has been unique to say the least, as I'm sure many of my media counterparts would attest. From keeping up with daily statistics to updating school plans and protocols — and juggling everything in between — there's never a dull moment in the life of a small-town news editor.

It has also taught me a lot. I've gleaned valuable lessons from each story and every interview. I've learned to be kinder, to count my blessings, to embrace change and to lend a listening ear to those with differing viewpoints.

I'm privileged to serve in a position that gives me the opportunity to capture historic moments our community will look back and reflect on for years to come. Reporting on such significant events — sometimes heartwarming and heartbreaking, other times cordial and controversial — has been a humbling experience.

The frenzied climate that kept my schedule full over the last 24 months hasn't changed much, but it's worth every pencil mark and scratch if it continues to keep area residents in the know.

REFLECTION

How has the pandemic reshaped how you live, interact with others and perceive the world? Take a moment to reflect on your handling of the changing world.

3

FAITH, FELLOWSHIP
& FORTITUDE

3:1
GROWING IN GRATITUDE
THROUGH HARDSHIPS

True character development comes by traveling
through the storm instead of rising above it.

We all went into 2021 with an elevated level of excitement but also a heightened sense of caution.

We didn't know what to expect entering a new season on the heels of a tumultuous 365 days wrought with social unrest, political division and a worldwide pandemic. We did know, however, that the end of 2020 would pave the way for a renewed outlook on life.

Of course, that restored perspective of the future came only by choice, not by chance. Each of us were left with a decision to either adopt a positive mentality going into the forthcoming months or not; I can only hope that most of us did.

Twenty-twenty handed me an unexpected office closure,

a positive COVID-19 diagnosis and a divorce (albeit an amicable one) — not to mention the dozens of other challenges that came with normal, everyday life.

Fast-forward to today, and the light at the end of the tunnel doesn't seem so distant; in fact, it appears quite close. And my slow journey out of the shadows hasn't been paved with regret and destruction, but it's been cemented, rather, with growth and gratitude.

If there's one thing I've learned along the way, it's that true character development comes by traveling through the storm instead of rising above it. We're often trained to avoid confrontation, elude uncomfortable situations and embrace convenience, but these all eventually lead to a life of complacency and resentment.

Take it from me, allowing certain tests and trials to strengthen — rather than stifle — our resolve will only go to better ourselves and others around us. What's more, choosing to be thankful in the midst of the turmoil is a true testament of ongoing self-improvement.

My theme in 2021 — "growing in gratitude" — came, for example, from a more trivial experience dealing with a noisy, nocturnal upstairs neighbor after moving into my new apartment. When the clock struck midnight, his "day" suddenly began. Let's just say that a quiet night's sleep wasn't in the cards for me anytime soon.

One night after awakening for the 100th time, however,

my perspective unexpectedly shifted. I happened to glance at my ceiling, not with the same scornful demeanor as before, but with a slight grin and a grateful spirit. Lying there, I thought, "I'm thankful I have this roof over my head." "I'm thankful I woke up in a warm, comfy bed."

I moved to another apartment shortly thereafter (I still needed sleep, after all), but I took what I learned through that experience — embracing an attitude of appreciation, especially when dealing with nuisances like inconsiderate neighbors — and am now applying it to other similar situations.

I'm now living in a quieter and calmer environment, sure, but I believe I had to experience a period of restless nights to fully appreciate those blessings (like a roof and bed) that I take for granted every day.

REFLECTION

*W*hat challenges or inconveniences are you facing that you need to reevaluate from a different perspective? Turning a negative into a positive can help us live a more peaceful life.

3:2
A BLACK MAN WHO BEFRIENDS WHITE SUPREMACISTS

'Take the time to sit down and talk
with your adversaries.'

I recently watched an inspirational video about a Black man who has devoted his life to breaking down the walls of racial divide by befriending members of the Ku Klux Klan.

Daryl Davis started attending KKK rallies in the mid-1980s, where he would stand and listen to the group's speeches and observe their rituals. After many of the meetings, he would approach different Klansmen, shake their hands and join them for dinner on the grounds of the rallies.

There, they would engage in meaningful conversations about their differences, with Davis asking questions, taking notes and even sharing a laugh or two with the members.

In the video, broadcast by TEDxNaperville, Davis shares his

experiences with a large crowd, and highlights the importance of approaching difficult discussions with a mutual regard for other people's worldviews.

"Respect is the key, sitting down and talking, not necessarily agreeing, but respecting each other to air their points of view," he tells attendees. "Take the time to sit down and talk with your adversaries; you will learn something, and they will learn something from you."

Davis' efforts to connect with those who rallied against him led the longtime R&B and blues musician, activist and author to establish a personal relationship with KKK Imperial Wizard Roger Kelly at the time. From there, the two became close friends, and Kelly eventually left the Klan and gave Davis his robe.

Davis claims to have been directly responsible for collecting between 40 and 60 robes from former Klansmen, which came as a result of his willingness to simply listen, ask questions and engage with them.

"When two enemies are talking, they're not fighting," Davis says in the video. "It's when the talking ceases that the ground becomes fertile for violence, so keep the conversation going."

It goes without saying that the challenges of the last several years have led to an upheaval of racial and political divide, the likes of which many of us have never seen before. From rioting in the streets to hateful discourse on social media, our nation has grown more polarized with each broken store window and offensive Facebook post after the next. Our focus has shifted to glaring at someone's mask — or lack thereof — rather than what's in their eyes. We spend our time rebuking others for how they voted instead of asking them why they did. Assuming the worst about our adversaries rather than wishing them the best has become commonplace.

Instead of inciting violence or eliciting an angry response, perhaps our best course of action during turbulent times is to take a page out of Davis' book and invest in those who don't share our same worldview — especially those we haven't even met.

Davis said it best in his TED talk, referencing the first time he experienced racism at an early age: "It was inconceivable to me that someone who had never laid eyes on me, never spoken to me ... would want to inflict pain upon me for no other reason than the color of my skin."

His lack of understanding at the time could have led him to down a path of pain and resentment. However, he chose to embrace a life of compassion and understanding, which he used as a way to later convert the very same people who persecuted him.

It's time to listen, ask questions and take notes. It's time to be willing to hear others' opinions before declaring our own. It's time to learn and grow together. Davis did, and he was faced with insurmountable odds.

REFLECTION

When's the last time you stopped and listened to — and internalized — someone else's opinions? Connecting with them despite your disagreements could change your life and theirs.

3:3
KEEPING UP WITH PESKY, YEAR-ROUND RESOLUTIONS

> *What happens to that passion? Where does all that gusto end up going?*

Resolutions are often associated with New Year's, but we all know how well those plans turn out.

We hype ourselves up, share our gallant goals with others and start out strong with our heads held high. Somewhere along the line, however, we fall short, and our enthusiastic shouts of "I can't wait to…" quickly turn into apathetic claims of "I'll just wait until next year…"

What happens to that passion? Why do we get halfway through February and call it quits? Where does all that gusto end up going?

Before you paint me as a pessimist, allow me to elaborate a bit and say I'm horrible with resolutions — both making them and sticking to them — so this narrative is reflective of those failures.

At the same time, I wish I was better, and perhaps writing this will play into that improvement process. So, allow me to share a few of my "year-round" resolutions, which I hope to see through beyond just the beginning of a 365-day cycle.

I'd like to work out more. Yes, I know, everyone has that same goal, but for me, I haven't (voluntarily) visited a gym in, oh, about a decade or so. I certainly don't want to find myself saying those same words a decade from now.

I want to start eating more healthily. Of course, this goes hand-in-hand with the latter, but it's just so darn hard to put those sweets down. Perhaps I should start by closing this open bag of Keebler Fudge Stripe Cookies I've been munching on for the last 10 minutes.

I'd like to finish a work of fiction. I've tried my hand at several short stories, none of which I've actually completed or published. There's just something about coming home and writing after a long day of writing that doesn't seem that appealing.

I want to read more. I have books galore on every subject, from self-help and spiritual inspiration to mystery and science fiction, and I haven't picked up one in quite a long time. My excuse? TV, chores, writing, you name it. I probably need to stop writing this so I can start this resolution.

I'd like to be more of a handy man. I have more of a desire to hone my craft behind the comfort of a tidy desk than I do to get my hands dirty learning the ins and outs of a leaky faucet or broken toilet. Maybe that's why my water bill is so high.

Or perhaps I should forget all of these and make my main resolution to be better at making resolutions.

On a more serious note, I want to be a better all-around man: a better son to my parents, a better leader to my colleagues, a better friend to others and a better member of my church and my community.

REFLECTION

I encourage you to strive to continue creating and carrying out different resolutions throughout all times of the year.

3:4
SCALING A STEEPER
MOUNTAIN

I'll take pride in braving the terrain behind my desk as an adventurous writer.

I may not be the rescuer of repairs or the cowboy of construction, but I do like to consider myself an aspiring mountain man (or at least lend credence to the fleeting thought).

If you're unfamiliar with the show "Mountain Men," it's an American reality TV series on the History Channel that follows the simplistic yet rugged lifestyles of eight men and their families who reside in different backcountries and "live on the land."

Some areas the show covers include the Alaskan Ridge, New Mexico's Cimarron Valley, Great North Woods in Maine, Snake River and Teton Range in Idaho, Montana's Ruby Valley and the Blue Ridge Mountains of North Carolina.

The families build their own houses and structures; hunt,

kill and eat all their own food; use ancient techniques to harvest various resources; and even develop and teach basic wilderness survival skills — all without the use of modern technology and with little to no contact with the outside world.

In all, it's a program that makes regular guys like me who watch it want to do all the ultra-macho things they do. But it also strikes up the question, "Do I really have what it takes?"

Like many men broaching the same subject, I have my share of doubts.

The more I watch this show, the more inadequate I feel knowing I'm not necessarily called to be a "mountain man," but more so a "wimpy writer" who lives out his days typing words on a computer rather than hunting game on a hilltop.

It's easy to base my identity on something as simple — and shallow — as a TV show, especially when those characters resemble what I believe to be the pinnacle of a real man. In fact, I've oftentimes sought validation through these personality types.

But deep down, I know that just isn't true.

In his book "Killing Lions," John Eldredge states, "Our starting place is to ask God what he thinks of us, to allow our Father to speak to us as sons. Then from there we begin to get active in the process of seeking and receiving (true) identity and validation."

For too long, I've strayed from seeking selfhood in God, only to come up short looking for affirmation elsewhere, and

Eldredge's words are an important reminder that it's time to hear — and accept — what Jesus says about who I am in Him. Colossians 3:9-10 states, "I have put off the old man and have put on the new man, which is renewed in the knowledge after the image of Him who created me." Philippians 4:13 also says, "I can do all things through Christ who strengthens me."

Based on these passages, I'm made in the image of God, and I have what it takes.

It's in Christ alone — and not a TV show — where I can find my true sense of self. What a relief knowing I don't have to seek validation in my own strength and in something that will always leave me empty and wanting more.

I'm sure one day I'll get my chance to scale the vast terrain of the wilderness as a rugged "mountain man," but for now, I'll take pride in braving the terrain behind my desk as an adventurous writer.

REFLECTION

*W*hat validates your sense of self? Where do you seek validation? Perhaps a recalibration of what defines your
identity is in order.

3:5

BUILDING BRIDGES
RATHER THAN BURNING THEM

> *It's best to tuck that match back into the box before igniting it over a petty grievance or past mistake.*

L ife has a funny way of reminding us that we inhabit a small world.

One thing I've learned in my 36 naïve years on this giant rock is that everything comes full circle, and building more bridges than burning them has proved to be a wise choice in nearly every situation.

Of course, watching the flames from afar can sometimes serve as a cheap thrill (until the dust settles and cleanup begins), but I digress.

It seems these days that someone knows at least someone else who knows you, and that can be a blessing or a curse, depending on how many overpasses you've set ablaze in the past.

Let's just hope there are more standing than not.

We've all unwittingly walked into that awkward encounter with an old friend or colleague at the grocery store. Smiles are thrown in both directions, topped with a clichéd "How are you?" a forced "It's great to see you" and an obligatory "We should get coffee sometime."

All the while, both parties are silently recalling the smoke, the piles of debris, the lumber left in pieces, the watery grave of a once popularly traversed walkway (and that coffee never gets scheduled, does it?).

Revisiting a collapsed bridge at the grocery store is one thing, but carrying that into the office, a local city meeting or even church takes the level of regret to a new level.

A lot of us run in close-knit circles here in a small-town community, and it goes without saying that everyone knows everyone — and that includes the next person who probably knows your pastor, boss, friends, parents, the list continues.

In other words, it's best to tuck that match you've been eager to strike back into the box before igniting it over a petty grievance or past mistake. Choose, rather, to grab a hammer and some nails and get to work fortifying a stable footpath.

Thankfully, I've come to appreciate and preserve a good bridge: one that can withstand any heated sparks over the test of time.

REFLECTION

How are you working toward continuing to build more bridges than burning them? What past bridges that you've destroyed can you rebuild?

3:6
MOON LANDING
STILL RESONATES WITH US

> *Here's to us pushing beyond our limits, scaling the heavens and exploring the unknown.*

July 2019 marked 50 years since we set foot on the moon.

The moon landing — and the whole "space race" era — has always fascinated me. Although I wasn't alive then, the endeavors of those in cockpits and control rooms resonate in my heart today.

I've often found myself glued to the screen watching footage of this remarkable time, mesmerized at the scale of human achievement that can only be described as awe-inspiring.

Hard-working men and women dedicated a good part of a decade — away from family and friends, sacrificing the everyday normalcies and niceties that we all take for granted — to embark on a journey of historic proportions.

I look back in envy at many of these individuals who had a hand in lettering the history books: charting a course for orbit, securing the bolts to a rocket booster, operating a countdown clock, scaling a ladder to the lunar surface.

It goes without saying that they made the impossible possible.

Remnants of the Apollo missions — and the earlier Gemini and Mercury programs — are now imprinted on launch pads down the coast of Cape Canaveral in Florida and enshrined in museums and exhibits across the country.

Fifty years later, the efforts of those courageous men and women at the helm of one of America's greatest achievements will never be forgotten. Their passion and perseverance have paved the way for a host of feats that may not have been realized if it weren't for their choice to act.

From the twin Voyagers to the Space Shuttle and International Space Station to SpaceX and the Mars Curiosity Rover, our continued sojourns into space are certainly not taken in vain.

I often find myself staring off into the night sky, fascinated, even haunted, by the vastness of the universe. But I glance back at the moon and envision Neil Armstrong's footsteps perfectly preserved in the Sea of Tranquility, still echoing, "... one giant leap for mankind."

Here's to us pushing beyond our limits, scaling the heavens and exploring the unknown.

REFLECTION

*H*ow are you pushing beyond your own limitations? You may not be the next person to step foot on the moon, but the sky's the limit when it comes to your potential.

3:7
CHOOSING IMMERSION
OVER ISOLATION

I had to devote a season to saying "yes" in moments when I felt like saying "no."

I went into 2022 wanting more of the same.

That may seem like a discouraging statement, but it's quite the contrary, especially since the latter half of 2021 lent to me making new friends and spending more time around others.

Following a tumultuous time dealing with divorce, the pandemic and the like, immersing myself in community — specifically a church community — has radically transformed my life. I may have initially veered off course seeking value in worthless pursuits, but eyeing faith and fellowship has steered me back to fullness.

I recently heard a podcaster discuss the concept of non-negotiables — actions we ideally should regularly prioritize that go toward enriching our minds, bodies and souls — and church-going has made its way to the top of my list.

Choosing immersion over isolation has helped me to navigate life's treacherous terrain with likeminded individuals.

Choosing immersion over isolation has led me to dust off my guitar to play for the worship team and grow more familiar with stage production in the sound booth.

Choosing immersion over isolation has given me the opportunity to serve and encourage other congregants.

Choosing immersion over isolation has paved the way for my healing and wholeness.

Of course, these same principles can be universally applied to life outside the church's four walls — regardless of one's faith or denomination — but my personal journey involves regular attendance at a local place of worship.

Coming out of complacency meant I needed to show up to every social gathering I could, lean into conversations and break through the barrier of discomfort naturally associated with meeting new people. It meant I had to devote a season to saying "yes" in moments when I felt like saying "no."

It took me 36 years to realize I'm worth surrounding myself with people who share a vested interest in contributing to my spiritual upkeep and vice versa.

Community is needed. Fellowship is essential. Immerse yourself. Get involved. Stay active. Embrace others. It truly is healing.

REFLECTION

How are you immersing yourself in community — especially spiritual community — during challenging times? Find a local church to call home.

4

AN ODE TO
OWASSO

4:1
LEARNING A LOT FROM
LOCAL LECTURERS

*Count me in as the first to rush through the door
and find a front-row seat.*

I've had the privilege of hearing several city and state officials speak at different events on a number of important topics, ranging from school funding to small business growth to community outreach.

Sitting down with these individuals — whether it be for a brief interview or a visit over a quick meal — I've noticed a common theme among each of them: They always have something to offer.

Filled with knowledge, passion and enlightenment, these people offer something they're convinced that we, as an audience, need to hear. Count me in as the first to rush through the door and find a front-row seat.

I enjoy listening, taking notes and asking probing questions when and where I can, especially while sitting in on a session that hosts a speaker who broaches a subject that's unfamiliar to me; it gives me an opportunity to grow.

Here in Owasso, we have superb programming stemming largely from the city and chamber, along with local charity organizations, churches and outreaches, school groups, small businesses and more. I'm honored to be on scene to cover these events and share the lecturers' many words of wisdom.

I've learned more than I expected after taking on the role here at the Reporter, all thanks to the extraordinary men and women of Owasso — and those special speakers visiting the community — who pour their heart and souls into teaching their spectators something new. I can only aspire to follow in their footsteps.

I encourage you to get out and attend some of these events throughout the community, to listen in and engage with those behind the podium and discover something new. There's a lot happening here and across the state that deserves our attention, and these forums are a great source of information. See you soon in one of the crowds.

REFLECTION

*H*ave you taken time to attend a local event lately? Perhaps a gathering at a local business recently struck your interest. Attend, engage and learn something new.

4:2
THE PLEDGE OF ALLEGIANCE: A SACRED TRADITION

I'm proud to be a part of a community that upholds this sacred tradition.

I pledge allegiance to the Flag of the United States of America, and to the Republic for which is stands, one nation, under God, with liberty and justice for all."

We all (I hope) know the Pledge of Allegiance by heart. Time and again, American citizens have recited this 31-word patriotic oath in classrooms and community events as an expression of their loyalty to their country.

The Pledge, written by Baptist minister Francis Bellamy in 1892, was formally adopted by Congress in 1942 and has since become one of the most recognized — and revered — declarations in the world.

Over the years, however, the Pledge has come under criticism for its use of the words "under God" and has been met with controversial legal issues concerning its presence in public schools.

Despite these challenges, the Pledge has outlasted rebuke thanks to the thousands of citizens still upholding the hand-over-heart gesture at townships across the nation.

And Owasso is certainly no exception.

In my six-year tenure at the paper, I've had the privilege of attending a number of city and chamber meetings, among other events, where attendees proudly take part in the Pledge at the beginning of each assembly.

"Stand at attention, face the flag, salute." These words are routinely spoken with dignity and authority, leading attendees into the Pledge as first priority.

The moving sight of city leaders, businesspeople and involved citizens proclaiming their allegiance to the flag, to their country, in unison is enough to bring anyone to tears through its meaning and emotion.

The Pledge should always be respected and reverenced — never held in contempt or taken for granted — and Owassons have set a true example of how this should be followed that I've seen firsthand.

There's no doubt this city recognizes the importance of reciting the Pledge at every meeting, and I'm proud to be a part of a community that upholds this sacred tradition.

REFLECTION

*W*hy do you recite the Pledge of Allegiance? Is it important for you to stand and salute the American flag?

4:3
THE SOMBER AND PRAYERFUL
HEART OF OWASSO

This was a memory to preserve in the annals of Owasso's history.

I feel a recent photograph I took of Owasso's city manager bowing his head in prayer with his eyes firmly shut captured the heart of the Owasso community in the second half of 2021: somber, prayerful and hurting.

Attendees of Owasso Character Council's annual luncheon in October took a moment of silence to honor the loss of three Owasso police officers due to COVID-19.

Rapid clicks of my camera echoed throughout Tulsa Tech's Post Oak Room during the brief pause, but not without good reason; this was a memory to preserve in the annals of Owasso's history.

There was something about seeing the city manager —

136

and a roomful of his fellow community leaders — bow their heads in reverence to the memories of officers Howard Smith, Edgar "Buddy" Pales and Jose Romero that struck a chord with me.

Howard, a 21-year veteran of the Owasso Police Department, succumbed to the coronavirus on Sept. 27. Edgar, a 28-year member of the force, died Aug. 29. And Jose, a former reserve officer who served at OPD from 2003 through 2016, also passed away in Florida on Sept. 7.

These three victims of the pandemic were far from forgotten at the Council's luncheon, and their legacies will continue live on in our memories for years to come.

I wasn't close to Buddy or Jose, but I shared a unique bond with Howard over the years — one that mostly involved him throwing me a comical glance every time I pointed the camera his way; he was always a hoot in front of the lens.

The last photograph I took of Howie was at a memorial service for Owasso police K-9 Samson in August. I shot about a half-dozen candids of him goofing off before finally getting him to pose in front of a bouquet of flowers — a testament to his humorous, lighthearted spirit.

I'm going to miss Howard's humor and the positive energy he brought to every event that led us to cross paths, including Samson's service. He always greeted me with a smile and an amusing comment that never failed to make me laugh. He would always quip with, "There's a front-pager" or "I hope you got my good side," after each snap of the camera.

I'm sure Buddy and Jose also graced my lens at different times over the years — albeit unbeknownst to me — but I'm confident I captured them at their happiest serving the residents of the community that they loved.

I wasn't able to bow my head during the luncheon's moment of silence, but I hope capturing those who did at least gave Howie, along with Buddy and Jose, a further sense of peace looking down on all of us.

I think it goes without saying that Samson isn't alone upstairs anymore. He now has three of Owasso's finest at his side, looking after his well-being for the rest of eternity. I'm sure that would make for a great picture — one that Howie would probably have something witty to say about.

REFLECTION

*W*ho has passed that once graced your lens? How are you honoring them and their loved ones?

4:4
A CITY OF STRONG
RESILIENCE AND RESOLVE

We have stayed the course, remained
unfazed and pressed forward.

Ambitious and accomplished. Striving and steadfast. Call Owasso what you will, but words like these, in my opinion, encapsulate the very heart of this community.

And much can be said about the Owasso area's ongoing expansion and engagement as well.

There's always an event to cover, a resident to spotlight, a business to recognize, an accolade to present. It's no secret that Owasso is a rich hotbed of noteworthy — and, of course, newsworthy — happenings.

I'm reminded of this every week when I venture into the field to capture all the goings-on of the community, recording residents' voices, their actions, their expressions, their stories

— a true testament to Owasso's resilience.

And nowhere has this been demonstrated more than in the face of adversity over the last few years. In the throes of a global pandemic, political divisiveness and everything else in between, we have stayed the course, remained unfazed and pressed forward.

That's not to say we haven't experienced hardships. We've struggled to make ends meet; we've lost friends and relatives to COVID; we've seen tragedies unfold both domestically and overseas. But the heart of the community remains steadfast and undeterred.

Residents of this character-driven city join with countless others across the country and offer up their support and prayers in the face of adversity. It's their deep-rooted dedication and loyalty to each other that serves as a firm reminder to those struggling that they're not alone.

I sometimes feel like a broken record when I write these columns commending my fellow Owassons. But I can't say enough about the upstanding community that we are and that we will continue to be.

And that goes for the residents of Collinsville as well. My regular ventures up to Owasso's northernmost neighboring town are always filled with fond memories of kind gestures and meaningful conversations.

So this is a simple "thank you" to those who go above and beyond to make this a city that looks after its own. After all, if a global pandemic — and all the uproar it has brought with it — can't stifle our resolve, nothing can.

REFLECTION

How has your hometown given back to you, and how have you returned the favor? Perhaps that cycle is the very recipe for resilience.

ABOUT THE AUTHOR

*A*rt Haddaway is the editor of the Owasso Reporter. He has served at the helm of the small-town Oklahoma newspaper for six years. Art graduated from Oral Roberts University in 2008, where he earned a Bachelor of Arts in Mass Media Communication. He is a graduate of Leadership Owasso, a member of Workforce Owasso and an ambassador for the Owasso Chamber of Commerce, and also serves on the Oklahoma Press Association Education Committee. Art has earned 18 honors and awards during his journalism career. When he's not putting pen to paper as a local newsman, Art can be found serving in the worship arts department at his church, First Baptist Owasso.

Bringing new adventures to life, one word at a time.

www.designvaultpress.com

Made in the USA
Monee, IL
15 March 2022

92494819R00090